IMPERIAL SERVICE TROOPS

A group representative of the Imperial Service Troops maintained by the feudatory Princes of India, and including men of many of the races and tribes already touched upon in these notes. These troops are held at the disposal of the King-Emperor in case of need, and, when called upon, take their place with the British-Indian Army. The total of this force is very considerable, aggregating approximately fifteen regiments of cavalry and twelve battalions of infantry, to which must be added mountain batteries, some companies of sappers, and valuable transport corps (both mule and camel). The Imperial Service Troops thus form not only a notable and splendid testimony to the loyalty of the feudatory Princes and peoples, but also a fighting force of great value.

INDIA AND THE WAR

WITH AN INTRODUCTION

BY

LORD SYDENHAM OF COMBE
G.C.S.I., G.C.M.G., G.C.I.E., F.R.S.
FORMERLY GOVERNOR OF BOMBAY

WITH 32 ILLUSTRATIONS

SECOND EDITION

HODDER AND STOUGHTON
NEW YORK AND LONDON
MCMXV

Printed in Great Britain by Hazell, Watson & Viney Ld.,
London and Aylesbury.

THE coloured illustrations of types of Indian troops are taken (by permission) from *The Armies of India*, painted by Major A. C. Lovett, Text by Major G. F. MacMunn, D.S.O. (A. & C. Black). The explanatory notes which accompany these pictures have also been compiled wholly or mainly from information contained in the same work, to which the fullest acknowledgment is made.

The uncoloured illustrations are taken (by permission) from *The Historical Record of the Imperial Visit to India* (John Murray).

5804

CONTENTS

PART I

INTRODUCTION

APPENDIX I

APPENDIX II

PART II

RAJPUTANA INFANTRY

This illustration shows men of various Rajput regiments. The Gujars, who are shown to the left, belong to a race believed to be of Scythian origin (like the Jats), who settled on the banks of the Indus and spread to Gujarat, Rajputana, and Delhi In the Punjab they ultimately adopted the Mahomedan religion. They have been enlisted only of recent years, but have proved a success as soldiers. In ordinary life they are mainly graziers, and the name is often used to denote the occupation rather than the race.

LIST OF ILLUSTRATIONS

IN COLOUR

IN HALF-TONE

LIST OF ILLUSTRATIONS

6TH KING EDWARD'S OWN CAVALRY AND 8TH CAVALRY

JATS

The Jats are a race spread over the whole of upper India. They are supposed to be of Scythian origin. They form a large proportion of the Sikh sect, but there are also many hundreds of thousands professing the creed of Islam, and also, besides these, many Hindus who call themselves Jats. They are an agrarian race—peasant farmers —but consider fighting the most honourable of professions. The greater part of the Sikhs who serve in our Indian Army are Jats.

PART I

INTRODUCTION

BRITISH RULE IN INDIA

HIS HIGHNESS AGA SULTAN SIR MAHOMED SHAH, AGA KHAN, G.C.S.I., G.C.I.E.

The Aga Khan has no territorial possessions, but is the spiritual head of the Khoja community of Mahomedans in Western India. He received the title of His Highness as a personal distinction in 1886, was created K.C.I.E. in 1898, G.C.I.E. in 1902, and G.C.S.I. in 1911.

The principal seat of the Aga Khan family is in Bombay. His Highness is highly educated and enlightened, is a good speaker, and has travelled widely. He has done much for his community and for the Moslem world generally, and is a great supporter of education.

Vernon.

His Highness the Aga Khan, G.C.S.I., G.C.I.E.

PART I

BRITISH RULE IN INDIA

THE establishment of British dominion in India has no parallel in the history of the world. The great Empires of ancient and modern times have been built up by conquests, successively consolidated and carried out overland from the source of central power. The latest of such Empires—that of Germany—was created in little more than 250 years by successful war in accordance with the deliberate designs of a ruling dynasty formerly based upon the ideal of a union of the German peoples and in recent years disastrously expanded into a claim to dominate Europe. British Rule in India has been won by the sea, and its growth from the period of maritime exploration

leading to small settlements on the coast-
line was an evolution brought about by the
operation of inexorable forces.

In the internal conditions which existed
in India in the eighteenth century, it was
inevitable that dominion must pass to the
Power which could assert and maintain
naval supremacy. Portugal, Spain, Holland,
and France had all contended for mastery,
and the decision, momentous to the destiny
of India, was reached in a long series of
Western wars by sea and land. Once secure
against the interruption of her maritime
communications with the East, Great Britain
might have proceeded to impose her dominion by systematic steps; but this was
not attempted, or contemplated. The occupation of Bengal, following the rout of
the Nawab at Plassey in 1757, and the
transfer of the Government of the East
India Company to Calcutta, marked the first
great steps in the direction of political
power. Not only were British resources

14TH MURRAY'S JAT LANCERS

Risaldar-Major

JATS

The Jats are a race spread over the whole of upper India. They are supposed to be of Scythian origin. They form a large proportion of the Sikh sect, but there are also many hundreds of thousands professing the creed of Islam, and also, besides these, many Hindus who call themselves Jats. They are an agrarian race—peasant farmers —but consider fighting the most honourable of professions. The greater part of the Sikhs who serve in our Indian Army are Jats.

so greatly increased that the position and prestige of the French in India were jeopardised, but the Power which was to prove strongest at sea obtained territory giving direct access to the vast plains and the great water-ways which stretch north-westward for 1,200 miles towards the Indus and the Hindu Kush. Bengal had been ruled for centuries by foreigners, and the capitals of the great conquering dynasties had been founded in the broad fertile regions watered by rivers fed from the Himalayan snows. But never before had the gate of this region been held by a Power which came by and drew its resources from across the sea. Clive had shown unerring military instinct ; but he cherished no project of dominion. Before returning to India in 1765 to deal with " the critical situation of the Company's affairs " [1] he wrote that—

" If ideas of conquest were to be the rule

[1] Dispatch of the Court of Directors to the Council in Bengal.

of our conduct, I foresee that we should by necessity be led from acquisition to acquisition until we had the whole Empire up in arms against us."

In the Resolution of the House of Commons [1] thanking Lord Wellesley after the defeat of Tippu, Sultan of Mysore, who had formed an alliance with the French to evict us from India—a defeat which " established on a basis of permanent security the tranquillity and prosperity of the British Empire in India "—Sir Alfred Lyall traced the sound of the first Imperial note.

No one can form a just judgment of the steps—for the most part absolutely inevitable—which led to the establishment of British Rule without some knowledge of the history of India and of the internal conditions of that country in the eighteenth century. Mongols, Aryans, Persians, Greeks, Scythians, Huns, Arabs, Afghans, Turks, and Moguls have in successive streams passed

[1] October 1799.

BHOPAL

HER HIGHNESS NAWAB SULTAN JAHAN BEGAM,
G.C.S.I., G.C.I.E., C.I., BEGAM OF BHOPAL

Bhopal is the principal Mahomedan State in the
Central India Agency, and ranks next in import-
ance to Hyderabad among the Mahomedan States
of India. It is bounded by the territories of
Gwalior and Indore, by several petty States of the
Central India Agency, and by British territory.

The area of the State is 6,902 square miles (a
little less than the size of Wales), the population
is 730,383, chiefly Hindus, and the yearly revenue
about 38 lakhs (£253,300).

The present ruler, Her Highness Nawab Sultan
Jahan Begam, G.C.S.I., G.C.I.E., C.I., succeeded
her mother in 1901, and has followed closely in the
footsteps of her eminent predecessors. She takes
an active part in directing the work of her officials,
and inquires personally into all grievances. In
education she is greatly interested, and maintains
numerous schools, including two large girls' schools
and an industrial school for widows.

Her Highness maintains a large body of Imperial
Service Troops, both cavalry and infantry.

Her Highness the Nawab Begam of Bhopal, G.C.S.I., G.C.I.E., C.I.

6]

into India. Some penetrated deeply, founding kingdoms and mixing in greater or less degree with the aboriginal inhabitants and with their predecessors. Almost all have left some mark upon the language, customs, and religions of the most heterogeneous aggregate of peoples to be found in the world. For seven hundred years India was subjected to recurring waves of warlike Mahomedans, who at length built up the most powerful state and dynasty that had existed prior to the coming of the British. " Asiatic dynasties," wrote Gibbon, " present one unceasing round of valour, greatness, discord, degeneracy, and decay," and before the death of Aurungzebe in 1707, the Mogul Empire had completed this round and was tottering to its fall. Upon its ruins arose the Maratha power which, surging from the south-west, took Delhi, occupied the Punjab, and strove for the mastery of Upper India. At Panipat in 1761, the Maratha army, which had attracted to itself hordes of armed freebooters, was routed by Ahmed Shah, who had invaded India through the passes of the north-west a year before. The Afghan leader made no attempt to create a new Moslem dynasty and soon withdrew his troops laden with spoils. The military power of the Marathas never recovered from this blow and degenerated into dangerous predatory forces which, after spreading devastation far and wide, were finally shattered in 1818. The effects of the breaking up of the Mogul Empire, which had exercised authority with growing inefficiency over a large portion of India, were catastrophic. In the pregnant words of Sir Alfred Lyall, the Indian people "were becoming a masterless multitude prepared to acquiesce in the assumption of authority by any one who could show himself able to discharge the most elementary functions of government in the preservation of life and property."

Such were the conditions existing over a vast territory, and out of the welter British

BIKANER

COLONEL HIS HIGHNESS MAHARAJA SIR GANGA
SINGH BAHADUR, G.C.S.I., G.C.I.E., A.D.C.,
LL.D. (CANTAB.), MAHARAJA OF BIKANER

Bikaner is one of the largest States of Rajputana,
in which it is situated near the States of Jodhpur
and Jaisulmer.

The area is 23,000 square miles (rather more
than three times the size of Wales), the population
is about 701,000, chiefly Hindus, and the yearly
revenue is about 41 lakhs (£273,400).

His Highness was born in 1880, succeeded his
elder brother in 1887, and was invested with full
ruling powers in 1898. He is second to no Indian
ruler in the enlightenment and efficiency of the
administration of his State, and is a keen soldier.

In 1901 he served with the British Forces in
China.

In the world of sport His Highness is well known
as a polo player, and has few equals as a shot,
both with gun and rifle. He is an A.D.C. to His
Majesty the King-Emperor of India.

Herzog & Higgins.

Colonel His Highness the Maharaja of Bikaner,
G.C.S.I., G.C.I.E., LL.D., A.D.C.

power gradually wrought peace and order. It is false to speak of the conquest of India. We found ourselves confronted by inexorable forces originating in the distant past— forces which combined to produce a state of anarchy unparalleled even in the blood-stained annals of India. Only a strong power brought to bear from the outside could have rescued the country from ruin. And when the stupendous task was accomplished, more than one-third of all India and one-fourth of the population was left, and remains to-day, under direct Indian rule. The existence of nearly 700 Native States, ranging from Hyderabad with more than thirteen millions of people to the hereditary domain of a small chief with not so many thousands, is often ignored in this country and is little realised elsewhere. Some of these States were rescued from chaos and re-created by the British Government,[1] to

[1] Thus the important State of Mysore was reconstructed under its ancient Hindu dynasty, and after a period of

2

which all owe the consolidation of their
power and the security of their territories.
The Queen's Proclamation in 1858 [1] gave the
promise that—

" We shall respect the rights, dignity, and
honour of the Native Princes as our own,
and we desire that they, as well as our own
subjects, should enjoy that prosperity and
social advancement which can only be
secured by internal peace and good government."

This promise, which was renewed fifty
years later by King Edward VII., [2] has been
faithfully kept, and the protected Princes
and Chiefs know well that the stability of
their historic houses and the maintenance
of their rights depend entirely upon the
strength of British Rule. They perfectly
understand that the triumph of Pan-
Germanism would involve anarchy through-

British administration ending in 1881 has prospered ex-
ceedingly under the wise Rule of the late and the present
Maharaja.

[1] Appendix I.   [2] Appendix II.

25TH CAVALRY (Frontier Force)

PATHAN

The Pathans claim for themselves, in common with the Afghans, a Jewish descent, the legendary ancestor being a certain Kais, said to have been 37th in descent from King Saul, and to have lived in the days of Mahomed. However this may be, Afghans and Pathans appear to be closely allied, and the latter dwell for the most part between the Indian border and Afghanistan, with some in Afghanistan itself and some within British territory. There are many tribes of them, among whom may be mentioned the Afridis and the Khattaks, both of whom make fine soldiers. The Pathans are of fierce temper, and much given to blood-feuds ; these quarrels are suspended while the men are on service, but promptly resumed on retirement or during furlough.

out India, and that the imposition of German methods of government, of which the guiding principle is that might is right, would rob them of all they hold dearest. They have one and all nobly responded, in the martial spirit of their ancestors, to the call of loyalty, and the wonderful announcement made by the Viceroy on their behalf is the most striking proof of their heartfelt devotion to the British Crown which has guaranteed their honour and their possessions.

Before leaving India in 1856, Lord Dalhousie, in prophetic words, pointed to the duties which remained to the British rulers.

" I trust," he said, " we shall still feel that all we have yet done must be regarded as no more than the first beginnings of greater things that are to come. In regions so vast as these and among interests so various, all progress must be gradual and slow."

The depredations of Marathas and Pindaris had been suppressed. British authority

had been extended to the geographical
frontier, and the process of consolidation
was making sure way, after a period of wars
frequently recurring, when the wild outbreak
raised by the Mutiny of the Bengal Army
threatened for a time to bring back the
age of anarchy. In 1858 the Government
of India was transferred to the Crown, and
for more than half a century the internal
peace of India has been kept secure. Only
when order had been restored and firmly
established on the basis of law and justice
could Government devote itself to the
" greater things " to which Lord Dalhousie
referred.

It is impossible here to give any idea of
the great work of ameliorisation which is
going on with increasing speed. Sir John
Strachey in his valuable book described the
machinery and methods of government.
The interesting studies of M. Chailley explain
the problems and the difficulties of administration on Western lines in an Eastern

country. That some mistakes should have been made was inevitable. No form of government is perfect, and mistakes as great as any perpetrated in India have occurred in countries where the problems are relatively simple. It can, however, fearlessly be claimed that the progress achieved in India has no parallel in similar circumstances.

The total permanent debt of British India on March 31, 1911, was £270,063,145, of which no less than £195,836,888 was incurred for public works (railways and irrigation), leaving £40,426,063 as ordinary debt. In 1857 there were about 300 miles of railway; the mileage now exceeds 33,000, and the benefits have proved immense. The great irrigation works commanded more than 16,000,000 acres in 1910–11, and have since been largely increased. In the Punjab especially, new towns have sprung up where formerly a sparse population led a precarious existence. Roads and bridges are being multiplied. The total sea-borne trade reached 260½ million pounds in 1911 with an excess of exports of 29¼ millions. For the same year the burden of taxation per head was 1s. 11½d., and including land revenue which, in accordance with the old custom of India, is not taxation, the amount was 3s. 7·1d. The cotton industry, which is mainly in Indian hands, increased the number of mills in ten years from 71 to 226, and new industries supported by Indian capital are springing up, while the mineral output shows marked development. In primary education there have been rapid advances in late years, and more than one-fourth of the boys of school age are receiving instruction, while slow but steady progress is being made with girls' schools, and needed reforms in higher education are being gradually accomplished. The results of the wonderful material progress of India have been the enrichment of large classes which in pre-British days had no chance of bettering

31ST DUKE OF CONNAUGHT'S OWN LANCERS

Daffadar

DEKKANI MAHRATTA

The Marathas or Mahrattas are the land-owning class of the Deccan—of the plateau and the seaboard of Western India. They first became famous under the chief Sivaji, who attempted to overthrow the Great Mogul and to establish a Hindu empire. Later in history they waged two great and obstinate wars against the British, the first famous, amongst other battles, for Wellington's victory at Assaye. They have long served with high distinction in the Bombay Army, and have a reputation for great wiliness and endurance. Several of the princely families of the old Mahratta confederacy still reign over feudatory States.

their position, the steady growth of purely
Indian enterprise, and the first beginnings
of an abandonment of the ancient system
of hoarding in favour of remunerative in-
vestment.   As in all countries similarly cir-
cumstanced, the cultivating classes suffer
when the rainfall fails over any large area.
In good years, there is probably no happier
or more contented peasantry in the world.
Such appalling periodic devastations caused
by famine as are recorded in the annals of
India have ceased.   Highly organised administrative methods aided by railways have
minimised the actual want in bad years,
and the tracts rendered immune by irrigation are being steadily increased.   Plague is
still a scourge, and the immense development of communications causes it to spread
more easily than in former days; but
prolonged researches have provided the
medical authorities with preventive measures,
and the inherited resentment of the people
against sanitary precautions shows signs of

abatement. Wages have everywhere increased, and Indians of middle age see marked evidence of a general improvement in the resources of the rural population.

The establishment of the *Pax Britannica* throughout India was accomplished mainly by Indian soldiers trained by British officers and supported by small bodies of European troops. The creation of the fine Native Army of India—a work of which any nation might be proud—was a growth from haphazard beginnings. " An ensign and thirty men " with " a gunner and his crew " representing British power in Bengal at the end of the seventeenth century, a small garrison sent to Bombay when it was at length transferred to the Crown as part of the dowry of Catherine of Braganza, and a few companies formed from factory guards at Madras were the seeds from which sprang the three great Presidential Armies ; but Dupleix in 1748 was the first to raise bat-

GWALIOR

MAJOR-GENERAL HIS HIGHNESS MAHARAJA
SIR MADHO RAO SCINDIA BAHADUR OF
GWALIOR, G.C.S.I., G.C.V.O., A.D.C., LL.D.
(CANTAB.)

The great State of Gwalior is the largest in the
Central India Agency, bounded on the east by
British districts, on the south by other Central
India States, and on the west by Rajputana.

The total area is 25,862 square miles (nearly three
and a half times the size of Wales), the population
is about 3,000,000, mostly Hindus, and the yearly
revenue is estimated at Rs. 1,64,00,000 (£1,082,500).

The present Maharaja succeeded in 1886 at the
age of ten years. Besides being a keen and able
soldier (he served on the staff of Sir A. Gaselee in
China in 1900), His Highness is a most enlightened
administrator. His energy is indefatigable, and he
devotes the closest personal attention to all the
details of the government of his vast estates. He
received the degree of LL.D. of Cambridge University in 1903. He is an A.D.C. to His Majesty
the King-Emperor of India. The Gwalior State
maintains several regiments of Imperial Service
troops, both cavalry and infantry.

Major-General His Highness the Maharaja Scindia of
Gwalior, G.C.S.I., G.C.V.O., LL.D., A.D.C.

talions of Mussalman troops drilled in European fashion in the Carnatic. In 1754 the first regiment of the British Army—the 39th Foot—arrived in India, and at the end of the eighteenth century the European forces belonging to the Royal and the East India Company's armies numbered about 13,000 men. The exigencies of war led to a rapid increase of Indian regiments, and when the Great Mutiny broke out, there were about 311,500 Native and 39,500 European troops in India. In many severe campaigns the Indian troops displayed great bravery under British leadership, and to the close relations between officers and men engendered on stricken fields our military success was due. Upon the mutual trust and affection existing between them the strength of the Indian Army depends to-day, and the stirring Order of the Day [1] issued by Lieut.-General Sir James Willcocks on October 10 expresses the con-

[1] See page 75.

fidence reposed in our gallant Indian soldiers by their commanders.

The old army of the Company rendered Imperial services in many parts of the world —Ceylon, Amboyna, Egypt, Macao, Bourbon, Rodriguez, Java, Persia, Afghanistan, Burma, and China. Indian troops as soldiers of the Crown have distinguished themselves in Abyssinia, Afghanistan, Egypt, the Sudan, Somaliland, Burma, and China, and were brought to the Mediterranean in 1885, while Indians in a non-combatant capacity rendered useful aid in the South African War. When the whirlwind of the Mutiny engulfed most of the Bengal regiments and drew into its vortex the classes over a large area which had resented the suppression of freebooting, the great mass of the people of India remained faithful to the Government. The small British forces employed never lacked willing assistance from Indians. The many Irregular Native Corps, hastily raised, played a great part

HYDERABAD

COLONEL HIS HIGHNESS ASAF JAH, MUZAFFAR-
AL-MULK WAL MAMALIK NIZAM-UL-MULK,
NIZAM-UD-DAULA, NAWAB MIR SIR USMAN
ALI KHAN BAHADUR, FATEH JANG, G.C.S.I.,
NIZAM OF HYDERABAD

Hyderabad, the principal Native State in India,
is situated in Southern India, and is bounded on
the north-east by the Central Provinces, on the
south and south-east by the Presidency of Madras,
and on the west by the Presidency of Bombay.
The area of the State is 82,698 square miles (more
than one and a half times the size of England), the
population is 13,374,676, and the average annual
revenue about 498 lakhs (£3,319,700). The State
was founded by one of the Generals of the Emperor
Aurangzeb in 1724.

The present Nizam is 29 years of age and
succeeded his father on August 29th, 1911.

The Nizam is entitled to a salute of 21 guns.
The State maintains two regiments of Imperial
Service Cavalry.

His Highness the Nizam of Hyderabad, G.C.S.I.

in breaking the rebellion, and the Bombay and Madras armies not only prevented it from spreading south, but rendered valuable assistance in the field. After 1858, the Indian Army was entirely reconstituted. The separate Presidency Armies, into which many differences of customs and equipment together with some abuses had crept, were abolished, and after a series of reforms the forces in India, with a stiffening of about 75,000 British troops, were organised as a Northern and a Southern Army under a unified system. Many of the historic regiments with a notable record of war service remain ; others date from the irregular corps created by British officers during the Mutiny. The long internal peace has tended to lessen the warlike qualities of some of the Indian races, and the present Army is drawn mainly from Northern India, exclusive of Bengal, the principal classes composing it being Punjabi, Hindustani or Deccani Mahomedans, Sikhs, Jats, Gurkhas, Hindu Rajputs,

Dogras, and Pathans. Such a classification gives no idea of the numerous clans comprised, each with some peculiar characteristic, custom, and prejudice of its own, illustrating the involved diversification of the Indian people which, in Northern India especially, corresponds to no geographical area.

The large armies formerly maintained by the Indian Princes have dwindled as the country became settled and agriculture increased ; but twenty-five Native States now provide contingents of Imperial Service Troops or Transport Corps well armed and equipped, and generously placed at the disposal of Government by their Rulers whenever needed. The Imperial Service Troops have rendered valuable services to the Empire in the past and they are now represented with the Allied Armies and in Egypt.

The splendid contingent which the Indian Army has given to the Imperial cause con-

38TH KING GEORGE'S OWN CENTRAL INDIA HORSE

Lance-Daffadar

GAKKAR (Punjabi Mussalman)

The Mahomedans of the Punjab (exclusive of the Pathan element) consist mainly of Hindu tribes who have at various periods accepted Islam. Some tribes claim a foreign origin, maintaining that they invaded and conquered the lands they occupy. Among these is the well-known military class of the Gakkars. The Punjabi Mahomedans supply many excellent soldiers to the Indian Army. They are enlisted in regiments according to their tribes, tribal pride and tribal traditions being thus preserved and promoted.

tains in its ranks descendants of the most
martial races of the world. The Rajputs
were renowned and chivalrous warriors when
Europe was emerging from barbarism. Their
military achievements cover a long period in
the annals of India. Rajput clans spread
far from the home of their power; but important States remain under the ancient
dynasties, and the heads of some great
historic houses are now serving the King-
Emperor in Flanders. Among the Mahomedan troops, there are descendants of the
great fighting races which swarmed into
India from the north-west; while others
have an Aryan ancestry, or represent the
sections of the peoples of India—Rajputs,
Brahmans, Jats, and Marathas—which em-
braced the Moslem faith. Mahomedans in
India are to a considerable extent non-racial.
The Sikhs, among whom Jats preponderate,
have no common ethnical affinity. They are
the adherents of a reformed Hinduism, first
preached by Baba Nanak of Lahore in the

latter half of the fifteenth century, and since spread widely among the Hindu clans of the Punjab and especially among the cultivating (Jat) population. The early adherents of the new religion suffered greatly at the hands of the Mahomedans; but, out of persecution, grew the great military sect which after the fall of the Mogul Empire established a short-lived kingdom in the Punjab. The Sikhs, our sturdy opponents in two wars, gave valuable assistance in the Mutiny and have since been largely recruited. The maintenance of their military qualities and of the purity of their religion is due in great measure to their incorporation in the Indian Army.

Under British rule, the Marathas have settled down into peaceful cultivators and their instincts as horsemen have been lost; but they supply six infantry battalions to the Army, and they have lately distinguished themselves at the head of the Persian Gulf. Dogras include Brahmans, Rajputs, and Jats

INDORE

HIS HIGHNESS MAHARAJADHIRAJA TUKOJI
   RAO HOLKAR BAHADUR, MAHARAJA OF
   INDORE

The Great Maratha State of Indore lies to the
north and south of the Norbada river in the
Central India Agency. It consists of several
isolated tracts which border on British territory,
on Rajputana, and on numerous other States of
Central India. The total area is 9,500 square
miles (about one-third the size of Scotland), the
population is 1,079,074, mostly Hindus, and the
yearly revenue about 76 lakhs (£507,000).

His Highness the Maharaja is now in his 25th
year. He takes great interest in all his State
affairs as well as in world politics. He is a good
horseman and shot, and excels at various games,
especially lawn tennis. He has lately played in
the Riviera championship tournament with A. F.
Wilding, the well-known Australian player.

The State maintains an Imperial Service Transport Corps.

W. E. Gray.

His Highness the Maharaja Holkar of Indore.

who did not embrace either Islam or the Sikh religion. They come mainly from Jammu, a feudatory State of the Maharaja of Kashmir, who descends from a Dogra Rajput family. Gurkhas and Hazaras are drawn from outside of British India. The former, Mongolian in early origin, are largely intermixed with other races and form several clans under a Rajput dynasty. They were first recruited after the Nepal War of 1814, and their fine soldierly qualities have been often proved in the field. The 2nd Gurkhas, which recently suffered severe losses near Ypres, shared with the 60th Rifles the honour of holding the exposed flank of the little army which, from the Ridge at Delhi, dealt the first great blow to the mutineers.

The Pathan tribes of the north-west borderland are divided into numerous clans who claim a Jewish descent, but have no racial homogeneity, although their barren mountainous country with its severe climate has given them common characteristics. They are born fighters, hardy and vigorous, and frequently at war with each other. The Pathans, originally confined to irregular corps, have been enlisted—Afridis especially —in considerable numbers in recent years, and their great endurance, marching power, and alertness as scouts fit them admirably for mountain warfare.

This brief sketch can give little idea of the many elements which compose the unique Army of India. Never before have so many races, so widely differing, been brought together in a great military organisation and united in the bonds of a common loyalty. The fine forces which the King-Emperor reviewed at Delhi in 1911, the Princes and Chiefs, some of whom can trace their lineage far back into the dim history of old India, and the vast masses of simple, kindly people who showed the most touching devotion to their Majesties, combined to presage the spontaneous rally of our Indian

JAIPUR

MAJOR-GENERAL HIS HIGHNESS SARAMAD-I-
RAJAHA-I-HINDUSTAN RAJ RAJINDAI SRI
MAHARAJADHIRAJA SIR SAWAI MADHO
SINGH BAHADUR G.C.S.I., G.C.I.E., G.C.V.O.,
LL.D., MAHARAJA OF JAIPUR

The State of Jaipur lies in the north-east and east of Rajputana. Its area is 15,579 square miles (more than twice the size of Wales); the population is 2,636,647, and the annual average revenue is about 80 lakhs (£533,300). The present Maharaja was born in August 1862 and succeeded in September 1880. The title of Colonel of the 13th Rajputs was bestowed upon His Highness on September 2nd, 1904, and that of Major-General at the Coronation Durbar on December 12th, 1911. The degree of LL.D. was conferred on April 10th, 1908, by the University of Edinburgh. His Highness was invested with full powers in September 1882. He takes a prominent part in the administration of the State, and all important matters are disposed of by himself assisted by his council of 11 members. He enjoys a salute of 21 guns, of which four are personal. His Highness was one of the Indian Chiefs who were selected to attend His Majesty the late King-Emperor's Coronation in England. The State maintains an Imperial Service Transport Corps, which has been twice on active service, viz., during the Chitral and Tirah campaigns.

Johnston & Hoffman.

Major-General His Highness the Maharaja of Jaipur,
G.C.S.I., G.C.I.E., G.C.V.O., LL.D.

fellow-subjects to the British Crown in the
time of national danger. The late Admiral
Mahan could justly write that : " The testimony to the uprightness and efficiency of
her (Great Britain's) Imperial rule, given
by the strong adherence and support of
India and the Dominions, is a glory exceed-
ing that of pitched battle and overwhelming
victory." [1]

When the Government of India was transferred to the Crown in 1858, it was the wish
of Queen Victoria that her message to the
Indian people should " breathe feelings of
generosity, benevolence, and religious tolera-
tion," and these sentiments have inspired the
progressive changes which have since been
wrought into the administration. Provin-
cial Councils have been reconstituted to
enable Indians to occupy executive posi-
tions, and this system will in time be extended to all India. No administrative
post except that of Head of a Province is

[1] In October last.

now inaccessible to Indians, who also hold one seat in the Council of the Viceroy and two in that of the Secretary of State. Indian judges sit in all the High Courts, and the administration of justice is mainly in Indian hands. Full opportunities are given for the expression of Indian opinion upon all measures of Government, and every grievance alleged receives the most careful inquiry. A great system of local and municipal self-government, managed almost entirely by Indians, has been set up, and will gradually teach lessons of citizenship as it is understood in Western countries. British rule, impartial and impersonal in its action, though depending for success mainly upon the personal characteristics of its agents, and loyalty to one Sovereign remain the only cementing force amongst 313 millions of the most diversified people in the world—the only force which stands between them and anarchy deeper and darker than that which followed the break-up of the Mogul Empire.

RAJPUT REGIMENT

The word Rajput means literally " sons of princes "
or " of rulers." After the Aryan Hindu invaders
from the north had come into India, they gradually broke up into three great divisions—the
Kshattryas or soldiers, the Brahmans or priests,
and the Vaisiyas, or general civil population.
The first-named class, composed of the military
followers or clansmen of the chiefs, called themselves "Sons of Princes." To-day Rajputs are
to be found all over India, even as Brahmans
are—in the Punjab (where they have accepted
Islam, but none the less remain Rajputs), in
Nepal, and as far west as the Deccan. But the
term is generally used—and especially so far as
military use is concerned—to denote the Rajputs
of Rajputana and Delhi, towards the west, and
the Rajputs of Oudh towards the east. The
Rajputs of Rajputana are famous as horsemen,
those of Oudh as infantry. The Rajputs have
high military pride and a great record in military
history.

And only under British rule can the diverse and jarring elements of a country as large as Europe without Russia be gradually welded together in the bonds of a common nation-hood. This vital truth is grasped by the wisest of the Western-educated classes of India, who realise the nature of the work which has been accomplished in their midst. In the words of Nawab Nizamut Jung, High Court Judge of Hyderabad :

> Unmindful of their ancient name
> And lost to Honour, Glory, Fame,
>   And sunk in strife
> Thou found'st them, whom thy touch has made
> Men, and to whom thy breath conveyed
>   A nobler life !

To lead her people onwards and upwards is alike the mission of British Rule in India and the justification of its maintenance ; but, in the words of Lord Dalhousie, the "progress must be gradual and slow."

APPENDIX I

EXTRACTS FROM A PROCLAMATION BY THE QUEEN IN COUNCIL TO THE PRINCES, CHIEFS, AND PEOPLE OF INDIA (PUBLISHED BY THE GOVERNOR-GENERAL AT ALLAHABAD, NOVEMBER 1, 1858).

VICTORIA, by the Grace of God of the United Kingdom of Great Britain and Ireland, and of the Colonies and Dependencies thereof in Europe, Asia, Africa, America, and Australasia, Queen, Defender of the Faith.

Whereas, for divers weighty reasons, We have resolved, by and with the advice and consent of the Lords Spiritual and Temporal, and Commons, in Parliament assembled, to take upon Ourselves the Government of the Territories in India heretofore administered in trust for Us by the Honourable East India Company:

Now, therefore, We do by these Presents notify and declare that, by the advice and consent aforesaid, We have taken upon Ourselves the said Government; and We hereby call upon all Our

Subjects within the said Territories to be faithful and to bear true Allegiance to Us, Our Heirs, and Successors, and to submit themselves to the authority of those whom We may hereafter, from time to time, see fit to appoint to administer the Government of Our said Territories, in Our name and on Our behalf.

We hereby announce to the Native Princes of India that all Treaties and Engagements made with them by or under the authority of the Honourable East India Company are by Us accepted, and will be scrupulously maintained; and We look for the like observance on their part.

We desire no extension of Our present territorial Possessions; and while We will permit no aggression upon Our Dominions or Our Rights to be attempted with impunity, We shall sanction no encroachment on those of others. We shall respect the Rights, Dignity, and Honour of Native Princes as Our own; and We desire that they, as well as Our own Subjects, should enjoy that Prosperity and that social Advancement which can only be secured by internal Peace and good Government.

We hold Ourselves bound to the Natives of Our Indian Territories by the same obligations of Duty which bind Us to all Our other Subjects; and those Obligations, by the Blessing of Almighty God, We shall faithfully and conscientiously fulfil.

Firmly relying Ourselves on the truth of Christianity, and acknowledging with gratitude the solace of Religion, We disclaim alike the Right and the Desire to impose our Convictions on any of Our Subjects. We declare it to be Our Royal Will and Pleasure that none be in any wise favoured, none molested or disquieted by reason of their Religious Faith or Observances; but that all shall alike enjoy the equal and impartial protection of the Law : and We do strictly charge and enjoin all those who may be in authority under Us, that they abstain from all interference with the Religious Belief or Worship of any of Our Subjects, on pain of Our highest Displeasure.

And it is Our further Will that, so far as may be, Our Subjects, of whatever Race or Creed, be freely and impartially admitted to Offices in Our Service, the Duties of which they may be qualified by their education, ability, and integrity, duly to discharge.

We know, and respect, the feelings of attachment with which the Natives of India regard the Lands inherited by them from their Ancestors; and We desire to protect them in all Rights connected therewith, subject to the equitable demands of the State; and We will that generally, in framing and administering the Law, due regard be paid to the ancient Rights, Usages, and Customs of India.

15TH LUDHIANA SIKHS

The Sikhs are not, correctly speaking, a race, but a religious sect, which includes a large proportion of the Hindu tribes and races of the Punjab. They form a military-religious order, professing a reformed Hinduism, on which later teachers (gurus) grafted a military organisation. The name itself means " disciple." The faith of the Sikhs has spread to most of the Hindu tribes of the Punjab, but the Jats form the predominating element. The wars against the Sikhs were among the most stubborn and critical of those which the British had to fight in India. In the Mutiny, however, the Sikhs remained faithful to the British, and rendered splendid service. They are tall, well-made men, of great courage. They wear their hair unshorn, though concealed beneath their turbans, and curl their beards and whiskers. By the rules of their faith they are forbidden to smoke tobacco

It is Our earnest Desire to stimulate the peaceful Industry of India, to promote Works of Public Utility and Improvement, and to administer its Government for the benefit of all Our Subjects resident therein. In their Prosperity will be Our Strength; in their Contentment Our Security; and in their Gratitude Our best Reward. And may the God of all Power grant to Us, and to those in authority under Us, Strength to carry out these Our Wishes for the good of Our people.

APPENDIX II

PROCLAMATION OF THE KING-EMPEROR TO THE PRINCES AND PEOPLES OF INDIA, READ BY HIS EXCELLENCY THE VICEROY IN DURBAR AT JODHPUR ON NOVEMBER 2, 1908

It is now fifty years since Queen Victoria, my beloved mother, and my August Predecessor on the throne of these realms, for divers weighty reasons, with the advice and consent of Parliament, took upon herself the government of the territories theretofore administered by the East India Company. I deem this a fitting anniversary on which to greet the Princes and Peoples of India, in commemoration of the exalted task then solemnly undertaken. Half a century is but a brief span in your long annals, yet this half-century that ends to-day will stand amid the floods of your historic ages, a far-shining landmark. The proclamation of the direct supremacy of the Crown sealed the unity of Indian Government and opened a new era. The journey was arduous, and the advance may have sometimes seemed slow; but the incorporation of many strangely diversified

JAMMU AND KASHMIR

MAJOR-GENERAL HIS HIGHNESS SIR PRATAP
SINGH BAHADUR, G.C.S.I., G.C.I.E., MAHA-
RAJA OF JAMMU AND KASHMIR

His Highness is a Dogra Rajput, and is 64 years
old.

He has a salute of 19 guns. His State covers an
area of 80,000 square miles (about one and a half
times the size of England). It has a population of
3,158,126. It stretches from the plains of the
Punjab to the watershed of the Himalayas, and
can boast of every variety of climate and scenery.

His Highness takes a great interest in the administration of his State.

The Imperial Service Troops maintained by the
State took part in the Hunza (1888) and Chitral
(1895) expeditions, and rendered valuable services
on each occasion.

Major-General His Highness the Maharaja of Jammu
and Kashmir, G.C.S.I., G.C.I.E.

communities, and of some three hundred millions of the human race, under British guidance and control has proceeded steadfastly and without pause. We survey our labours of the past half-century with clear gaze and good conscience.

Difficulties, such as attend all human rule in every age and place, have risen up from day to day. They have been faced by the servants of the British Crown with toil and courage and patience, with deep counsel and a resolution that has never faltered nor shaken. If errors have occurred, the agents of my Government have spared no pains and no self-sacrifice to correct them ; if abuses have been proved, vigorous hands have laboured to apply a remedy.

No secret of empire can avert the scourge of drought and plague, but experienced administrators have done all that skill and devotion are capable of doing to mitigate those dire calamities of Nature. For a longer period than was ever known in your land before, you have escaped the dire calamities of War within your borders. Internal peace has been unbroken.

In the great charter of 1858 Queen Victoria gave you noble assurance of her earnest desire to stimulate the peaceful industry of India, to promote works of public utility and improvement, and to administer the Government for the benefit of all resident therein. The schemes that have been

5

diligently framed and executed for promoting your material convenience and advance—schemes unsurpassed in their magnitude and their boldness —bear witness before the world to the zeal with which that benignant promise has been fulfilled.

The rights and privileges of the Feudatory Princes and Ruling Chiefs have been respected, preserved, and guarded; and the loyalty of their allegiance has been unswerving. No man among my subjects has been favoured, molested, or disquieted, by reason of his religious belief or worship. All men have enjoyed protection of the law. The law itself has been administered without disrespect to creed or caste, or to usages and ideas rooted in your civilisation; it has been simplified in form, and its machinery adjusted to the requirements of ancient communities slowly entering a new world.

The charge confided to my Government concerns the destinies of countless multitudes of men now and for ages to come; and it is a paramount duty to repress with a stern arm guilty conspiracies that have no just cause and no serious aim. These conspiracies I know to be abhorrent to the loyal and faithful character of the vast hosts of my Indian subjects, and I will not suffer them to turn me aside from my task of building up the fabric of security and order.

Steps are being continuously taken towards

JODHPUR

HONORARY MAJOR-GENERAL HIS HIGHNESS
MAHARAJADHIRAJA SIR PRATAP SINGH
BAHADUR, G.C.S.I., K.C.B., A.D.C., LL.D.
(CANTAB.), REGENT OF JODHPUR

His Highness is 68 years of age.

The numerous distinctions which he has received testify to the great value of the services which he has rendered to the Empire. His Highness, who was Regent of Jodhpur for his nephew in 1895, voluntarily assumed that duty again in 1911 on the latter's untimely death. From 1902 to 1911 he was Maharaja of Idar, which is now administered by his adopted son.

He served in the Tirah campaign and the Mohmand expedition, and held the command of the Imperial Service Lancers in China. His dignities include those of G.C.S.I., K.C.B., and LL.D. He is an Aide-de-Camp to His Majesty the King-Emperor of India.

As a soldier the Maharaja is a splendid example of the traditional courage and loyalty of the ancient Rajput blood, and is famous as a horseman, a polo player, and a sportsman. In spite of his years he insisted on serving in person with the British Expeditionary Force.

Jodhpur is one of the three chief States of Rajputana, and the Maharajadhiraja is the head of the Rathar clan of Rajputs. The area of the State is 34,963 square miles (one and one-sixth times the size of Scotland); the population is 2,057,553, and the average annual revenue about 72½ lakhs (£483,250).

The present Maharajadhiraja Sumer Singh was born on January 15th, 1898. His Highness being a minor has not been invested with ruling powers.

Major-General His Highness Maharaja Sir Pratap Singh,
Regent of Jodhpur, G C.S.I., G.C.V.O., K.C.B., A.D.C.

34]

obliterating distinctions of race as the test for access to posts of public authority and power. In this path I confidently expect and intend the progress henceforward to be steadfast and sure, as education spreads, experience ripens, and the lessons of responsibility are well learned by the keen intelligence and apt capabilities of India.

From the first, the principle of representative institutions began to be gradually introduced, and the time has come when, in the judgment of my Viceroy and Governor-General and others of my counsellors, that principle may be prudently extended. Important classes among you, representing ideas that have been fostered and encouraged by British rule, claim equality of citizenship and a greater share in legislation and government. The politic satisfaction of such a claim will strengthen, not impair, existing authority and power. Administration will be all the more efficient if the officers who conduct it have greater opportunities of regular contact with those whom it affects, and with those who influence and reflect common opinion about it. I will not speak of the measures that are now being diligently framed for these objects. They will speedily be made known to you, and, will, I am very confident, mark a notable stage in the beneficent progress of your affairs.

I recognise the valour and fidelity of my Indian troops, and at the New Year I have ordered that opportunity should be taken to show in substantial form this, my high appreciation, of their martial instincts, their splendid discipline, and their faithful readiness of service.

The welfare of India was one of the objects dearest to the heart of Queen Victoria. By me, ever since my visit in 1875, the interests of India, its Princes and Peoples, have been watched with an affectionate solicitude that time cannot weaken. My dear Son, the Prince of Wales, and the Princess of Wales, returned from their sojourn among you with warm attachment to your land, and true and earnest interest in its well-being and content. These sincere feelings of active sympathy and hope for India on the part of my Royal House and Line only represent, and they do most truly represent, the deep and united will and purpose of the people of this Kingdom.

May Divine protection and favour strengthen the wisdom and mutual goodwill that are needed for the achievement of a task as glorious as was ever committed to rulers and subjects in any State or Empire of recorded time.

DOGRAS

The Dogras come from the hills between the Punjab and Kashmir. They are of the old Aryan Hindu stock. They have never accepted Islam, nor on the other hand joined the Sikh movement. Though they have been enlisted in large numbers only in recent years, the Dogras are very highly valued as soldiers for their good behaviour, high courage, and great physical endurance. Besides those in British service, the feudatory State of Jammu and Kashmir maintains a force of Imperial Service Troops consisting mainly of Dogras, and these served with much distinction in the Chitral campaign.

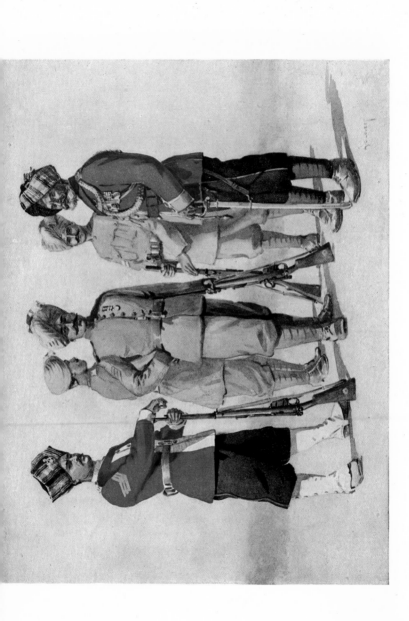

PART II

INDIA'S RALLY TO THE DEFENCE OF THE EMPIRE

KISHANGARH

MAJOR HIS HIGHNESS SIR MADAN SINGH BAHADUR, K.C.S.I., K.C.I.E., MAHARAJA OF KISHANGARH

His Highness is a Rathar Rajput and is 30 years old. His State covers 858 square miles and his subjects number 88,000. The annual revenue is estimated at about $8\frac{1}{2}$ lakhs (£56,660). He has a salute of 15 guns. His State was founded in 1594 by Kishan Singh, second son of Maharaja Udai Singh of Jodhpur. He served with distinction for over two years in the Imperial Cadet Corps. He was entrusted with ruling powers in December 1905. His Highness was made an honorary Captain in His Majesty's Army in March 1908 and an honorary Major at the Coronation Durbar on December 12th, 1911.

Herzog & Higgins.

Major His Highness the Maharaja of Kishangarh,
K.C.S.I., K.C.I.E.

INDIA'S RALLY TO THE DEFENCE OF THE EMPIRE

THE spontaneous outburst of loyalty from all parts of India on the outbreak of the war is shown in the documents that follow, and needs no elaboration.

MESSAGE FROM THE KING-EMPEROR TO THE PRINCES AND PEOPLES OF INDIA, SEPTEMBER 8, 1914

TO THE PRINCES AND PEOPLES OF MY INDIAN EMPIRE :

During the past few weeks the peoples of My whole Empire at Home and Overseas have moved with one mind and purpose to confront and overthrow an unparalleled assault upon the continuity of civilisation and the peace of mankind.

The calamitous conflict is not of My seeking. My voice has been cast throughout on the side of peace. My Ministers earnestly strove to allay the causes of strife and to appease differences with which My Empire was not concerned. Had I stood aside when, in defiance of pledges to which My Empire was a party, the soil of Belgium was violated, and her cities laid desolate, when the very life of the French nation was threatened with extinction, I should have sacrificed My honour and given to destruction the liberties of My Empire and of mankind. I rejoice that every part of the Empire is with me in this decision.

Paramount regard for treaty faith and the pledged word of rulers and peoples is the common heritage of England and of India.

Among the many incidents that have marked the unanimous uprising of the populations of My Empire in defence of its unity and integrity, nothing has moved me more

KOLHAPUR

HIS HIGHNESS SIR SHAHU CHATTRAPATI
MAHARAJ, G.C.S.I., G.C.I.E., G.C.V.O., LL.D.,
MAHARAJA OF KOLHAPUR

Kolhapur claims the first rank among States in the
Bombay Presidency, and the Ruler, descended
from the younger branch of Shivaji the Great, the
founder of the Mahratta Empire, bears the dis-
tinctive and honorific title " Chattrapati Maharaj."

The present Maharaja was born on June 26th,
1874, and succeeded on March 17th, 1884. The
area of his State is 3,165 square miles (nearly
twice the size of Somersetshire), the population 910,011, and the average annual revenue
about 49 lakhs (£326,600). His Highness enjoys
a salute of 21 guns, two of which are personal.
He received the title of G.C.S.I. in 1895 and the
title of G.C.V.O. in 1903. His Highness attended
the Coronation ceremony of the late King Edward
and was decorated with the insignia of the G.C.I.E.
by the King-Emperor at the Delhi Durbar in December 1911.

The administration of the State is markedly
efficient and His Highness takes a keen interest in
every detail.

His Highness the Maharaja of Kolhapur, G.C.S.I.,
G.C.I.E. G.C.V.O., LL.D.

than the passionate devotion to My Throne expressed both by My Indian subjects, and by the Feudatory Princes and the Ruling Chiefs of India, and their prodigal offers of their lives and their resources in the cause of the Realm. Their one-voiced demand to be foremost in the conflict has touched My heart, and has inspired to the highest issues the love and devotion which, as I well know, have ever linked My Indian subjects and Myself. I recall to mind India's gracious message to the British nation of goodwill and fellowship which greeted My return in February 1912 after the solemn ceremony of My Coronation Durbar at Delhi, and I find in this hour of trial a full harvest and a noble fulfilment of the assurance given by you that the destinies of Great Britain and India are indissolubly linked.

6

Offers of Service and Money

I received yesterday a summary of offers
of service and money made in India to the
Viceroy. The rulers of the Indian Native
States, numbering nearly 700 altogether,
have with one accord rallied to the defence
of the Empire and offered their personal
services and the resources of their States.
From among the many Princes and nobles
who volunteered for service in the war the
Viceroy has chosen the Chiefs of Jodhpur,
Bikaner, Kishangarh, Rutlam, Sachin, and
Patiala, Sir Pertab Singh (Regent of Jodhpur), the Heir Apparent of Bhopal, and a

brother of the Maharaja of Cooch Behar, together with other Princes belonging to noble families. The veteran Sir Pertab Singh, in spite of his seventy years, refused to be denied the right of serving the King-Emperor in person and is himself going to the front, accompanied by his great-nephew, the reigning Maharaja, who is only sixteen years of age and who was brought up at Wellington College. These have already joined the Expeditionary Force.

There are twenty-seven States in India that maintain Imperial Service Troops, and immediately on the outbreak of war the services of all of those corps were placed at the disposal of the Viceroy. From twelve of those States the Viceroy has accepted contingents of infantry, cavalry, sappers, and transport, and also the Bikaner Camel Corps; and some of those have already embarked on active service. Further than that, a number of Chiefs, entirely of their own volition, combined to provide a hospital ship to be named *The Loyalty*, for the use of the Expeditionary Force. The Maharaja of Mysore has placed a sum of Rs. 50 lakhs [1] at the disposal of the Government for expenditure in connection with the Expeditionary Force. The Viceroy adds that the Maharaja of Gwalior, besides sharing in the expenses of the hospital ship—the idea of which was started by himself and that eminent lady the Begum of Bhopal—has placed large sums of money at the disposal of the Government of India for the purpose of providing a great number of horses as remounts. From Mahomedan Loharu in the Punjab and from two States in Baluchistan there are offers of camels with drivers to be supplied and maintained by the Chiefs and the Sirdars of those States. The Maharaja of Rewa, a distinguished Chief in Central India, has offered his troops, his treasury, and even his private jewellery to be placed at the disposal of His Majesty the

[1] About £333,333, or $1,600,000.

33RD PUNJABIS

Subadar

PUNJABI MUSSALMANS

This regiment is recruited from those Hindu tribes of the Punjab which have accepted the Mahomedan religion, and which have been already mentioned in the note on the Gakkars. This illustration shows them to be men of very fine physique.

King-Emperor.   I ought to add that a number of Chiefs, the Maharaja of Kashmir, the Maharaja of Bundi, besides the Maharaja of Gwalior, the Maharaja of Indore, and the Maharaja of Orchha, have besides independently subscribed large sums to the Fund of His Royal Highness the Prince of Wales. The Maharaja of Kashmir gave a large subscription to the Indian Fund, and, what will seem to your Lordships rather a new departure in the case of an Indian Prince, presided at a meeting of 20,000 people held at Srinagar and himself delivered a stirring speech, as the result of which large subscriptions were collected. The Maharaja Holkar offers, free of charge, all the horses belonging to his State forces which the Government may find it convenient to accept. The Nizam of Hyderabad has made a similar offer, as also have the Jam of Jamnagar and some of the other Bombay Chiefs. The Viceroy adds that every Chief in the Bombay Presidency has placed the whole of the resources of his State at the disposal of Government.

Then we go further afield. The Mehtar of Chitral—a name which evokes memories of quite a different kind—and the various tribes in the Khyber Agency have sent loyal messages and offers of support to His Excellency's Government.   All States, however remote, and some of the quite small States, have expressed their desire to give such assistance as they can. The Viceroy goes on to say, very truly, that last but not least, outside India altogether, generous offers of assistance were received from the Nepal Durbar.   The Nepal Government have placed the whole of their military resources at the disposal of the British Government, and the Prime Minster offered a sum of Rs. 3 lakhs [1] to the Viceroy for the purchase of machine guns or field equipment for some of the British Gurkha regiments, and also gave large donations from his private purse

---

[1] £20,000, or $100,000.

to the Indian Relief Fund and to the Prince of Wales's Fund.   He also offered Rs. 30,000[1] for the purchase of machine guns for the 4th Gurkha Rifles.

Then we go still further on to the heights. We find that the Dalai Lama has offered 1,000 Tibetan troops for service under the British Government.   He also states that innumerable Lamas all over Tibet are offering up prayers for the success of British arms.   In fact, there is only one spirit and one movement over the whole of India. The Viceroy has received thousands of telegrams and letters from every quarter expressing loyalty and the desire to assist; and the local administrations have also received a vast number.   They have come from every community, from all manner of different associations, religious and political, from all the different creeds, and from countless numbers of individuals offering their resources or their personal services.

[1] £2,000 or $10,000.

There have also been a number of enthusiastic offers of medical help, of some of which I hope we shall be able gratefully to avail ourselves. The Zemindars of Madras offered 500 horses at quite an early stage in the proceedings; and the Imperial Indian Relief Fund, which was started, of course, quite independently of any fund here, for the relief of distress caused in India itself, has been responded to with great enthusiasm and vigour. There were a certain number of Indian Chiefs in Europe at the time. These have not been any more backward in offering their assistance and help. I find that of those who were in these parts the Maharaja and the Maharani Maji Sahiba of Bharatpur subscribed to the Indian Relief Fund and offered the whole resources of their State to Government. The Raja of Akalkot, a Bombay Chief, offered his personal service; and the Raja of Pudukota placed his entire resources at the disposal of Government. The Gaekwar of Baroda

MYSORE

COLONEL HIS HIGHNESS MAHARAJA SIR KRISHNARAJA WADIYAR BAHADUR, G.C.S.I., MAHARAJA OF MYSORE

His Highness is a Kshatriya (Hindu) and is 30 years old. He succeeded his father in February 1895, and was invested with full administrative powers in August 1902. His State covers an area of 29,500 square miles (about the size of Scotland), has a population of 5,449,800, and the average annual revenue is about 236 lakhs (£1,573,180). He has a salute of 21 guns.

His Highness personally controls all the branches of his administration, and is a very capable and enlightened ruler. He maintains a large force of Imperial Service Troops.

Barton.
Colonel His Highness the Maharaja of Mysore, G.C.S.I.

48]

placed at our disposal the whole of his troops and the resources of his State. The son of the Mir of Khaipur, a Mahomedan Ruler in North-West India, offered his personal service. And I find also that of the British-Indian residents in this country a great number, young and old, have shown their one desire to offer some form of assistance—personal service, or medical service, or some form of contribution to the Empire—in a most loyal and generous manner.[1]

Proceedings in the Legislative Council

This afternoon I received a telegram from the Viceroy describing what happened yesterday at the meeting of his Legislative Council at Simla. The Viceroy tells me that,

[1] Further offers of help were subsequently announced, notably that of His Highness the Nizam of Hyderabad, who offered a contribution of 60 lakhs of rupees (£400,000) towards the cost of the war, and, in particular, to defray the entire expense while on foreign service overseas of his own regiment of Imperial Service Lancers and of the 20th Deccan Horse (of which he is honorary Colonel).

7

in opening the proceedings, the members stood while he conveyed to them the message from the King. The Viceroy made a speech, in which he said that he was sure he was expressing the views of the Council and of the whole of India in assuring His Majesty of unflinching loyalty and devotion. He went on to dwell upon the causes which led up to the war and the wicked and wanton manner in which it had been thrust upon the British Empire, and he explained the whole-hearted efforts which had been made by Sir Edward Grey for the preservation of peace so long as such preservation was possible. He expressed, of course, on his own account also, the warmest gratitude for the attitude of the people of India which has been described in what I have just stated to your Lordships. Then when the Viceroy had concluded, Mr. Chitnavis, representing the Indian community, expressed the gratefulness which they all felt for His Majesty's Message, and asked the Viceroy to assure

39TH GARHWAL RIFLES

The Garhwalis, or inhabitants of the Garhwal, a hill district west of Nepal, somewhat resemble the Gurkhas and used to be enlisted in Gurkha regiments, but are now formed into separate battalions, though retaining the Gurkha rifle uniform, as shown in the illustration. The Khasias are the best fighting race among them, but they all make good soldiers. In physique they are short, like the Gurkhas, but not so thick-set.

His Majesty that the whole country was with him in this hour of crisis and would loyally and devotedly do everything possible to ensure the success of the British arms. He then moved the following resolution :

"That in view of the great war, involving most momentous issues, now in progress in Europe into which our August Sovereign has been forced to enter by obligations of honour and duty, to preserve the neutrality guaranteed by treaty and the liberties of a friendly State, the members of this Council, as voicing the feeling that animates the whole of the people of India, desire to give expression to their feelings of unswerving loyalty and enthusiastic devotion to their King-Emperor and an assurance of their unflinching support to the British Government. They desire at the same time to express the opinion that the people of India, in addition to the military assistance now being afforded by India to the Empire, would wish to share in the heavy financial burden now imposed by the war on the United Kingdom, and request the Government of India to take this view into consideration and thus to demonstrate the unity of India with the Empire. They request His Excellency the President to be so good as to convey the substance of this Resolution to His Majesty the King-Emperor and His Majesty's Government."

That was seconded by one of the principal Mahomedan leaders, the Raja of Mahmudabad, who made an important speech. It was supported by one of the Punjab Sardars, and was further supported in an eloquent speech by Mr. Malaviya, one of the leading representatives of Indian opinion. It was also supported by a distinguished Mahomedan gentleman, Sir Fazalbhoy Currimbhoy, who speaks for Bombay; by Mr. Ghuznavi, speaking for the Mahomedans of Eastern Bengal; and by Mr. Banerjee, who is well known as an exponent of liberal views in

Bengal.   Mr. Banerjee, in supporting the Resolution, pointed out that—

" It was the duty of the Council to focus the sentiments of support and enthusiastic loyalty by which every province of the Empire was animated. They desired to tell the world, the enemies of England and all else whom it might concern, that their loyalty was not lip-deep, but that behind the serried ranks of one of the finest armies of the world were the vast and multitudinous races and peoples of India bound together as one man."

The Viceroy replied, and the resolution was carried without a single dissentient.

I think, my Lords, that we must all agree that this demonstration of true and heartfelt loyalty in India to the King-Emperor and to the Government is one of the most gratifying facts as the outcome of the present war. As we all know, the devotion and the offers of support from the self-governing Dominions of the Crown have been not less striking.

Those Governments are manned by people of our own blood, with countless memories and traditions which centre round these islands. But it is, perhaps, even more striking, certainly not less gratifying, that those who speak for the various races in India—races which represent a civilisation of almost untold antiquity; races which have been remarkable in arms, in arts, and in the science of government—should in so whole-hearted a manner rally round the British Government, and, most of all, round the person of their Emperor at such a moment as this; and I am certain that this House will desire to express, through those of us who are entitled to speak for it, its appreciation of their attitude and our recognition of the part that they have played and are playing.

45TH RATTRAY'S SIKHS

JAT SIKHS

This regiment is composed of men of Jat race who belong to the Sikh sect. The Jats form, perhaps, two-thirds of the Sikhs, and probably make the most valuable soldiers of all the Sikhs.

Comments of the Indian Press

The " Tribune " (*Lahore*)

We are prepared to make these sacrifices and more at the proper time. And here we would make one suggestion. If any troops are to leave this country for active warfare in Europe, let Indian as well as British soldiers be sent without distinction of race and creed to serve side by side in defence of our united cause. If Indian troops are sent on these terms, there will be unbounded enthusiasm in India. Let there be no question of " prestige " or the inadvisability of employing brown against white soldiers. Prestige must be based on conduct and on no other considerations.

The " *Bengalee* " (*Calcutta*)

Behind the serried ranks of one of the finest armies in the world, there stand the multitudinous peoples of India, ready to co-operate with the Government in the defence of the Empire, which, for them, means, in its ultimate evolution, the complete recognition of their rights as citizens of the freest State in the world. We may have our differences with the Government—and what people have not?—but in the presence of a common enemy, be it Germany or any other Power, we sink our differences, we forget our little quarrels and close our ranks, and offer all that we possess in defence of the great Empire, to which we are all so proud to belong, and with which the future prosperity and advancement of our people are bound up.

NAWANAGAR

HIS HIGHNESS JÀM SHRI RANJITSINHJI
VIBAHAJI, JAM SAHEB OF NAWANAGAR

Nawanagar is one of the first-class States in the Kathiawar Agency under the Government of Bombay. It is about the same size as Devon and Somerset, and has a population of 337,000. The annual revenue averages 22½ lakhs (£150,000). The State has an extended sea-coast, and supplies one squadron of Lancers to the Imperial Service Troops.

The present Chief is a Jadeja Rajput, and belongs to the same house as the Rao of Cutch. He is 42 years of age, and succeeded his cousin as Jam Saheb of Nawanagar on March 11th, 1907. He is entitled to a salute of 11 guns. He was educated at the Rajkumar College of Rajkot, and at Trinity College, Cambridge. He is the well-known cricketer. He first appeared for the Sussex County Club in 1895, and was champion batsman for All England in 1896 and 1900. He accompanied Stoddart's "All England" Eleven to Australia in 1897-98. He is the author of "The Jubilee Book of Cricket."

His Highness the Jam Sahib of Nawanagar.

The " Herald " (*Dacca*)

If the loyal meetings which are being held all over the country do nothing else, they will at least give the enemy to understand that Britain does not stand alone in the fight in which she had to enter much against her own will; and that the vast people of an Empire in which the sun never sets stand behind her like one man, ready to place at her disposal the last gun, the last man, and the last penny they possess.

The " Indian Patriot " (*Madras*)

The whole continent of India is moved by one feeling of concern and one feeling of loyalty and devotion. A united people of three hundred millions, merely standing behind the Government, imparts a moral stimulus and sense of strength which no enemy, however powerful, can disregard.

8

The " Beharee " (*Bankipore*)

India's fortunes are indissolubly linked up with those of England. As Lord Curzon rightly said, India cannot do without England, and England would be impotent without India. It is not implied that the mother-country has not enough men to fight the battles, or that it cannot unaided crush Germany. But the Indians and the Europeans in this country owe it to themselves to don the armour in defence of the Empire, to defend India, and, if need be, to go to any other part of the world at the call of the motherland.

The " Advocate " (*Lucknow*)

Now that England is at war with a foreign enemy she may absolutely depend upon the loyalty of the people of this country. They may have their grievances, they may have their differences with the Government, but

they are firmly attached to British rule ;
they are fully prepared at this crisis to place
their resources at the disposal of the authorities in defence of their country.

The " Jam-e-Jamshad " (*Bombay*)

This is the time when India should feel it
to be her duty to show to the world—to
England's foes and allies alike—how greatly
she is attached to her, how staunch and
resolute is her devotion to her interests, how
ready and willing she is to make any sacrifice
she can in men and treasure, for the defence
of her possessions and the assertion of her
honour and dignity

The " Gujarati " (*Bombay*)

Never in the history of British India has
there been such an outburst of enthusiastic
and fervent loyalty to His Majesty's Government as has been witnessed during the last

few days since Germany and Great Britain declared war upon each other and Europe thus became involved in the gravest complications. The Indian people have held meetings throughout the country to give expression to their sentiments of profound loyalty and offer Government such help and assistance as lie in their power. Hindus, Mahomedans, and Parsis have already offered and have resolved to offer prayers to the Almighty for the success of the British arms, and the whole country has as it were been moved to its depths by an overpowering consciousness of the impending danger. The deputation from the National Congress now in England have sent a letter to the English press, conveying to the King-Emperor an expression of their loyalty, emphasising that, whatever be the differences in times of peace, all Indians are united to Britain in times of war. Splendid offers of pecuniary help and even personal service by the Ruling Chiefs and Princes of India and Maharajas and

2ND KING EDWARD'S OWN GURKHA RIFLES (Sirmoor Rifles)

Subadar-Major

GURUNG GURKHA

The old kingdom of Gurkha was originally a comparatively small part of Nepal, but the term Gurkha is now applied to the majority of the inhabitants of Nepal. These comprise several races, both Aryan and Mongolian. The Gurung tribe is Mongolian. There are twenty battalions of Gurkhas in the service. The Gurkha soldiers, most of whom are short men though powerfully built, wear a rifle uniform and the old "Kilmarnock" cap, the universal army forage-cap of Crimean days. The Sirmoor Rifles (to which the officer in the illustration belongs) wear the same uniform as the British 60th Rifles, in memory of the fact of the two regiments having held the exposed flank of the Ridge of Delhi together throughout the Siege. The relations between the Gurkhas and the British soldiers—both officers and men—are extremely friendly, and the value of the Gurkhas as fighting men can hardly be exaggerated.

सु मे सन्तवीर ॐ २/२ गोर्खा

great Zamindars are being announced in rapid succession, and the whole country is animated with an ardent feeling of unswerving loyalty to the Throne and with a keen consciousness of the interdependence of all the parts of the British Empire. On the top of these demonstrations in the mofussil and in the sister provinces there was held at the Town Hall the largest and the most enthusiastic and representative meeting ever held in that hall. There is no doubt that the meeting and its proceedings presented the most memorable scene that has ever been witnessed in the historic Town Hall.

The Moslem "Hitaishi" (Calcutta)

The British Government has pledged itself that, though it is at war with Turkey, it will not attack our Holy Places nor permit the Russians or French to attack them; there is no reason for us to be anxious about it. Whatever may be the fate in store for Turkey in this war, there is no reason why Indian Moslems should make themselves uneasy. During the late Balkan war, when the European provinces of Turkey were one by one passing under the control of the Christians, even in those times of serious danger Turkey did not seek the help of the immense Islamic world for the preservation of her dominions, and it can never be possible that now that same Turkey will seek help when she has gone to battle in order to help Germany.

The British Empire is known as a Moslem Empire. For under no other sovereign on earth is there such a large Moslem population as under the British sovereign. In particular, no other sovereign is such a friend either of Islam as is the British sovereign. Such being the British Government, it is our bounden duty to show our sympathy for it in all ways during this time of danger.

Statements by Leaders of Indian Opinion

His Highness the Aga Khan, the spiritual head of a very important section of Mahomedanism and the most influential personage in Moslem affairs in India, when invited to express his opinion on the war and its effect on Indian Moslems, made the following declaration :

"The outpouring of Indian loyalty, which has so gratified the British people, is entirely in accordance with the traditions of Indian sentiment and loyalty, and with the expectations I formed when the clouds of war so suddenly gathered over Europe while I was visiting my followers in East Africa. I am confident that the spirit of devotion to the British cause thus exhibited will be maintained, whatever fluctuations may come in the fortunes of war before the righteous cause of the Allies is crowned with victory. The loyalty of the Indian Moslems to the King-Emperor is proof against any attempts of German diplomacy in the Near East or elsewhere to create a bastard pan-Islamic sentiment in favour of the ' mailed fist ' made in Germany.

" There is, however, no need to differentiate between the various communities, races, or localities of the Indian Empire. All classes, religions, and sections are united in eager support of the Imperial cause, and in gratification that their martial representatives are to assist, for the first time in history, in upholding that cause on the Continent of Europe. The decision to employ Indian troops is necessary, for it would have tended to chill the enthusiasm of the country if, as in South Africa at the beginning of the century, her sons had been denied the opportunity to prove on the battlefields of the West, as they have done so often in the

PATIALA

HIS HIGHNESS MAHARAJADHIRAJA SIR BHU-
PINDAR SINGH MAHINDAR BAHADUR,
G.C.I.E., MAHARAJA OF PATIALA

Patiala ranks first among the States of the Punjab, and is the senior of the three Sikh States known as the Phulkian States. It consists of three separate divisions, of which the largest lies south of the Sutlej river, the second is hill country stretching up to Simla, while the third is an isolated tract 180 miles from the capital on the borders of Rajputana. The total area is 5,412 square miles (about the size of Yorkshire), and the yearly revenue about 73 lakhs (£457,000). The population is about 1,500,000, of whom 55 per cent. are Hindus, the remainder chiefly Sikhs and Mahomedans.

His Highness Maharaja Sir Bhupinder Singh, who is now in his twenty-fourth year, succeeded in 1900 and was invested with full powers in October 1909.

He is well educated and takes a personal interest in his affairs; he is also athletic and a good cricketer.

The State maintains one regiment of Imperial Service Lancers and two regiments of Imperial Service Infantry.

His Highness the Maharaja of Patiala, G.C.I.E.

East, their fidelity to the King-Emperor.
This advance in the growth of Indian co-
operation in the responsibilities of Empire
will be another stone in the great landmark
of a beneficent Viceroyalty."

In the course of another speech His Highness said :

"He had always been convinced that Germany was the most dangerous enemy of
Turkey and other Moslem countries, for she
was the Power most anxious to enter by
'peaceful penetration' Asia Minor and
Southern Persia. But she had been passing
for years past as a sort of protector of Islam
—though Heaven forbid that they should
have such an immoral protector. Happily,
so far as the Moslem subjects of the King
were concerned, these efforts were absolutely
futile. They would never break down the
strong wall of their loyalty, which was
based on the consciousness that their dearest
interests, religious as well as civil, were
guaranteed to them by British rule more

9

securely than they could be by any other dominion. All Indians knew that if Britain was ever weakened India's aspiration, India's whole future would go to pieces. On the other hand, India was an inexhaustible source of man-power and wealth in natural resources to the British Empire. She asked no more in return than that the Queen's Proclamation of 1858 should be kept in the letter and the spirit."

Mr. Justice Abdur Rahim, an Indian Judge of the Madras High Court, wrote as follows to *The Times* on September 14 :

"We wish to avert by all that lies in our power the humiliation of a change of government. We have assurances afforded to us in the history of British occupation of India, by the promises of our Sovereign and the pledges given by British statesmen on solemn occasions, that the British Government in India has a higher purpose to serve than merely the maintenance of peace and order, which any Government must secure if it

TRAVANCORE

SRI SIR RAMA VARNA KULASEKHARA KRITHI-
PATI, G.C.S.I., G.C.I.E., MAHARAJA OF
TRAVANCORE

Travancore, the largest State under the political
control of the Madras Government, is bounded on
the east by the districts of Madura and Tinnevelly,
on the north by the Native State of Cochin and
the Coimbatore district, and on the west and
south by the Indian Ocean. It is one of the most
picturesque portions of Southern India. The area
of the State is 7,129 square miles (nearly the size
of Wales), the population 3,428,975, and the average
annual revenue about 138 lakhs (£919,900).

The present Maharaja was born in 1857, and in
1885 succeeded his uncle. He was created a
Knight Grand Commander of the Star of India in
1888 and a Knight Grand Commander of the Indian
Empire on New Year's Day, 1903. His Highness
was present at the Coronation Durbar at Delhi in
1911. He is entitled to a salute of 21 guns, two of
which are personal.

The administration of the State is carried on
under the authority of the Maharaja, and a popular
consultative Assembly has recently been con-
stituted.

His Highness the Maharaja of Travancore,
G.C.S.I., G.C.I.E.

is to exist at all. That purpose is to enlist by means of Western education the sympathy and co-operation of the people in the ideals of Western civilisation, so that they may ultimately be fitted to administer the affairs of their own country as an integral part of the British Empire. From the Germans we can have no similar guarantees. The progress in the desired direction may have been slow in the past, but we have every hope that the pace will now be considerably quickened ; this hope is greatly fostered by the recent administrative reforms with which Lord Morley's honoured name is associated, and by the sympathetic attitude of Lord Hardinge, our most popular Viceroy, towards national aspirations and sentiments. We believe that by remaining within the orbit of the British Empire we shall be able sooner to realise the destiny of India than otherwise. These are cogent reasons for our sinking all differences in the face of a common danger, apart from the apparent justice of the British attitude in this war."

Mr. Dadabhai Naoroji, a veteran of eighty-nine who has been closely connected with social and political work in India for the last sixty years or more, and was the first Indian to gain a seat as a member of the British House of Commons, wrote the following letter to *The Times* on September 5 :

"We are a people of the British Empire. Let us see what our duty and position is.

"If ever India expects to attain again her former glory, on the advanced character and scale of modern British civilisation, of liberty, humanity, justice, and all that is good, great, and divine, it shall be at the hands of the British people and with the British people as self-governing members of the British Empire.

"We are above all British citizens of the great British Empire, and that is at present our greatest pride. On the other hand, is

6TH GURKHA RIFLES

This picture shows men of another Gurkha regiment in their rifle uniform. The character of their physique—short and "stubby"—is clearly shown, as well as the Mongolian type of their heads.

Britain engaged in the present great struggle for some selfish purpose, for extension of her own dominion and power ?   No, it is simply for keeping her word of honour and for righteously discharging a solemn obligation for the peace and welfare of minor and weak Powers.

"Fighting as the British people are at present in a righteous cause, to the good and glory of human dignity and civilisation, and, moreover, being the beneficent instrument of our own progress and civilisation, our duty is clear—to do every one our best to support the British fight with our life and property.

"I have been all my life more of a critic than a simple praiser of the British rule of India, and I have not hesitated to say some hard things at times.   I can therefore speak with the most perfect candour and sincerity as to what the British character is, what the civilisation of the world owes to the British genius, and what we Indians owe to the

British people for benefits past as well as benefits to come.

"Yes; I have not the least doubt in my mind that every individual of the vast mass of humanity of India will have but one desire in his heart—viz. to support to the best of his ability and power the British people in their glorious struggle for justice, liberty, honour, and true human greatness and happiness.

"The Princes and people of India have already made spontaneous offers, and until the victorious end of this great struggle no other thought than that of supporting whole-heartedly the British nation should ever enter the mind of India."

The following is a letter from Mr. Bhupe-dranath Basu, who is closely connected with the movement of the Indian National Congress, and with various social and political activities in India :

"I have read with deep emotion—a sentiment which will be shared by all my country-

UDAIPUR (MEWAR)

HIS HIGHNESS MAHARAJADHIRAJA MAHARANA
SIR FATEH SINGHJI BAHADUR, G.C.S.I.,
G.C.I.E., MAHARAJA OF UDAIPUR

The area of the State of Udaipur (Mewar) in Rajputana is 12,691 square miles (more than one and a half times the size of Wales); the population is 1,293,776, and the average annual revenue about 26½ lakhs (£176,600). The Udaipur family is the highest in rank and dignity among the Rajput Chiefs in India. They belong to the Sesodia sect of the great Gehlot clan and it is their proud boast that they never gave a daughter to any Mahomedan Emperor. The Ruling Chief is considered by Hindus to be the representative of Rama, the ancient King of Ajodhya, by one of whose descendants, Kanak Sen, the present family was founded about A.D. 144. The present Chief was, on the death on December 23rd, 1884, of the late Chief without issue, unanimously selected for the *gadi* by the Maharanis and Sirdars. This selection having been accepted and confirmed by the supreme Government, His Highness was installed on March 4th, 1885, and was invested with full powers of administration on August 22nd, 1885. He was created a Knight Grand Commander of the Star of India in February 1887, and a Knight Grand Commander of the Indian Empire in December 1911. During the visit of Their Majesties to India for the Coronation Durbar in 1911 His Highness was appointed Ruling Chief in Waiting. The administration of the State is carried on under the personal supervision of His Highness the Maharana. His Highness is entitled to a salute of 21 guns, two of which are personal.

His Highness the Maharana of Udaipur,
G.C.S.I., G.C.I.E.

men, here and in India—the announcement
that Indian soldiers are to participate on
European soil in the world-wide struggle
now going on. We are grateful to the
Marquess of Crewe for the eloquent and
moving terms in which he referred to India
in his speech in the House of Lords. Representatives of an ancient civilisation and
possessed of an old-world chivalry and
valour, the Indian soldiers will not be
unworthy of the task to which they are
being called. For the first time they will
stand side by side with their British comrades against a common European enemy ;
for the first time the Indian people will
realise that they are trusted in the hour of
danger ; it is no time for looking back, but
for the first time we feel that we are truly
the equal subjects of the King.

"The noble Marquess has said that sufficient
safeguards have been provided against ex-
ternal or internal danger in India. There
is no fear of either. Whatever intrigues

Germany may stir up in Turkey, Moslem and Hindu in India are alike united in their unswerving devotion and loyalty to the Empire in this crisis. Nobody doubts, whatever may be the temporary difficulties, that we shall emerge victorious out of this terrible chapter in our history, and, if I may say so, in the history of England, brighter and nobler than any in the past, for now and henceforth England, India, and the Overseas Dominions will stand and grow together, united in bonds sanctified on the field of battle."

Mr. Surendranath Banerjea, another prominent leader of the Nationalist movement in India and twice President of the Indian National Congress, used the following words in seconding a resolution of loyalty at a meeting held in the Calcutta Town Hall on August 14:

" A slur had been cast upon the genuineness of Bengali loyalty. There were those who were never tired of pointing to Bengal as a speck in the Indian horizon, darkened by the presence of revolutionaries. This was a weapon in their hands. With them it was a plea to retard the cause of Indian advancement. These men, if they had eyes to see and ears to hear, should note the wave of loyal enthusiasm which within the last few days had swept over the country from one end to the other. If the revolutionaries could be counted by the handful, the loyal population could be reckoned by millions. What was the secret of India's loyalty ? Indians were loyal because they were patriotic. In the present circumstances of India, and for a long time to come, loyalty and patriotism were indissolubly linked together, acting and reacting upon each other and strengthening each other. Indians were loyal because, apart from the emotional side of it, they believe that with the stability and indeed the permanence of British rule were bound up the best prospect of Indian advancement. . . . Let all combine, young

10

and old, high and low, rich and poor, and maintain unsullied the ancient reputation of their country for duty and faithful service. Service rendered in this crisis would not be forgotten—it would be lovingly remembered —it would promote sympathy between the different parts of the Empire—it would strengthen the bonds of amity and goodwill between England and India and help forward the satisfactory solution of the many grave problems upon which the contentment, the happiness, and the prosperity of our people so largely depended.   Out of evil, good often cometh, and so in the dispensation of Providence this great calamity may help to forge a new bond of mutual love, of mutual esteem and of mutual regard between England and India, pregnant with vast possibilities of good to India and the Empire."

BIKANER CAMEL CORPS

RATORE RAJPUT

This man, a Rajput by race, belongs to the Camel Corps which forms part of the Imperial Service Troops maintained by the feudatory State of Bikaner. The Corps is five hundred strong, and has served in China and Somaliland.

Lieut.-General Sir James Willcocks' Message to the Indian Army Corps at the Front

Order of the Day, No. 1

Soldiers of the Indian Army Corps

We have all read with pride the gracious message of his Majesty the King-Emperor to his troops from India.

On the eve of going into the field to join our British comrades, who have covered themselves with glory in this great war, it is our firm resolve to prove ourselves worthy of the honour which has been conferred on us as representatives of the Army of India.

In a few days we shall be fighting as has never been our good fortune to fight before and against enemies who have a long history.

But is their history as long as yours ? You

75

are the descendants of men who have been mighty rulers and great warriors for many centuries. You will never forget this. You will recall the glories of your race. Hindu and Mahomedan will be fighting side by side with British soldiers and our gallant French Allies. You will be helping to make history. You will be the first Indian soldiers of the King-Emperor who will have the honour of showing in Europe that the sons of India have lost none of their ancient martial instincts and are worthy of the confidence reposed in them.

In battle you will remember that your religions enjoin on you that to give your life doing your duty is your highest reward.

The eyes of your co-religionists and your fellow-countrymen are on you. From the Himalayan Mountains, the banks of the Ganges and Indus, and the plains of Hindustan, they are eagerly waiting for the news of how their brethren conduct themselves when they meet the foe. From mosques and

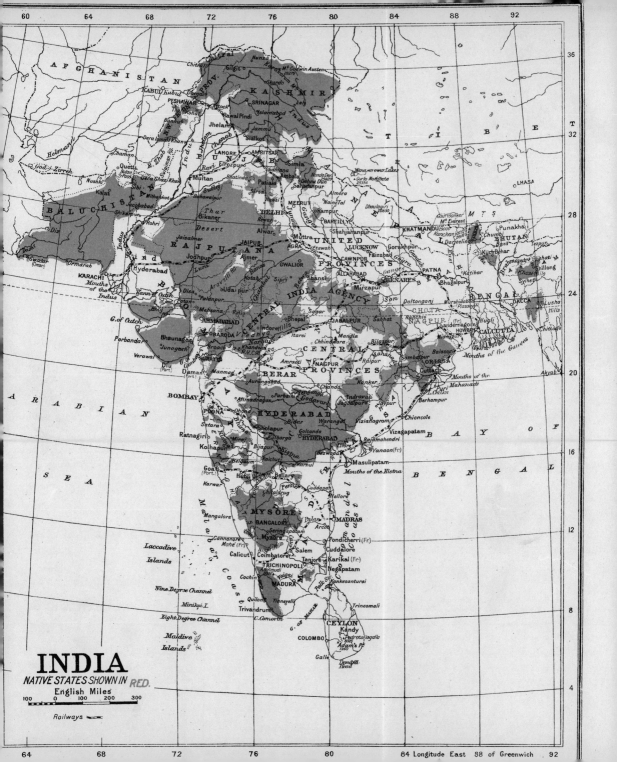

INDIA
NATIVE STATES SHOWN IN RED.
English Miles
Railways

temples their prayers are ascending to the God of all, and you will answer their hopes by the proofs of your valour.

You will fight for your King-Emperor and your faith, so that history will record the doings of India's sons and your children will proudly tell of the deeds of their fathers.

JAMES WILLCOCKS,

Lieut.-General,

Commanding Indian Army Corps.

CAMP,
October 10, 1914.

*Printed in Great Britain by Hazell, Watson & Viney Ld.,
London and Aylesbury.*